DISCOVERING
CAREERS FOR YOUR FUTURE

math

Ferguson Publishing Company
Chicago, Illinois

Carol Yehling
Editor

Beth Adler, Herman Adler Design Group
Cover design

Carol Yehling
Interior design

Laurie Sabol
Proofreader

Library of Congress Cataloging-in-Publication Data

Discovering careers for your future. Math.
      p. cm.
   Includes index.
   Summary: Describes the education, training, earnings, and outlook associated with twenty careers in the field of math, including auditor, bookkeeper, computer programmer, engineer, math teacher, and statistician.
   ISBN 0-89434-323-8
   1.Mathematics—Vocational guidance—Juvenile literature. [1. Mathematics—Vocational guidance. 2. Vocational guidance.] I. Title: Math

QA10.5 .D57 2000
510'.23—dc21

                                  00-022828

Published and distributed by
Ferguson Publishing Company
200 West Jackson Boulevard, Suite 700
Chicago, Illinois 60606
800-306-9941
www.fergpubco.com

Printed in the United States of America
Z-9

Table of Contents

Photo Credits

Astronomers, p. 11, *Mathew Hohmann*

Computer Programmers, p. 27, *IBM*

Computer Systems Analysts, p. 31, *IBM*

Engineers, p. 35, *Illinois State Water Survey*

Geophysicists, p. 47, *IBM*

Math Teachers, p. 51, *IBM*

Optical Engineers, p. 63, *Honeywell, Inc.*

Physicists, p. 67, *Honeywell, Inc.*

Software Designers, p. 71, *Carnegie-Mellon University*

Software Engineers, p. 75, *IBM*

Statisticians, p. 79, *Ron Veseley/Chicago White Sox*

Surveyors, p. 83, *Mathew Hohmann*

Introduction

You may not have decided yet what you want to be in the future. And you don't have to decide right away. You do know that right now you are interested in mathematics. Do any of the statements below describe you? If so, you may want to begin thinking about what a career in math might mean for you.

___Math is my favorite subject in school.

___I like to do work on math problems.

___I like number games.

___I like strategy games, such as chess.

___I like computers.

___I keep careful track of my money.

___I am curious about how things work.

___I am good at observing small details.

___I like to solve problems.

___I like science.

___I like to take things apart and see if I can put them back together.

___I like to invent things.

Math: Discovering Careers for Your Future is a book about careers in math, from actuaries to math teachers. Actuaries, software engineers, computer analysts, mathematicians, and statisticians are among the top ten careers listed in *Jobs Rated Almanac*. Math is important in dozens of careers in government, science, business, and industry. Computers, banking and finance, and engineering are all based on mathematics.

This book describes many possibilities for future careers in math. Read through it and see how different math careers are connected. For example, if you are interested in money and banking, you will want to read the chapters on Actuaries, Bank Services Workers, Bookkeepers, Financial Planners, and Computer Programmers. If you are interested in computers, you will want to read the chapters on Computer Programmers, Computer Systems Analysts, Software Designers, and Software Engineers. Go ahead and explore!

What do they do?

The first section of each chapter begins with a heading such as "What Demographers Do" or "What Mathematicians Do." It tells what it's like to work at a particular job. It describes typical responsibilities and assignments. You will find out about working conditions. Do they work in offices or laboratories? Do they use computers? What other tools and equipment do they use? This section answers all these questions.

How do I get there?

The section called "Education and Training" tells you what schooling you need for employment in each job—a high school diploma, training at a junior college, a college degree, or more. It also talks about on-the-job training that you could expect to receive after you're hired and whether or not you must complete an apprenticeship program.

How much do they earn?

The "Earnings" section gives the average salary figures for the job described in the chapter. These figures provide you with a general idea of how much money people with this job can make. Keep in mind that many people really earn more or less than the amounts given here because actual salaries depend on many different things, such as the size of the company, the location of the company, and the amount of education, training, and experience you have. Generally, but not always, bigger companies located in major cities pay more than smaller ones in smaller cities and towns, and people with more education, training and experience earn more. Also remember that these figures are current averages. They will probably be different by the time you are ready to enter the workforce.

What is the future for math careers?

The "Outlook" section discusses the employment outlook for the career: whether the total number of people employed in this career will increase or decrease in the coming years and whether jobs in this field will be easy or hard to find. These predictions are based on economic conditions, the size and makeup of the population, foreign competition, and new technology. Keep in mind that these predictions are general statements. No one knows for sure what the future will be like. Also remember that the employment outlook is a general statement about an industry and does not necessarily apply to everyone. A determined and talented person may be able to find a job in an industry or career with the worst kind of outlook. And a person without ambition and the proper training will find it difficult to find a job in even a booming industry or career field.

Where can I find more information?

Each chapter includes a sidebar called "For More Information." It lists organizations that you can contact to find out more about the field and careers in the field. You will find names, addresses, phone numbers, and Web sites.

Extras

Every chapter has a few extras. There are photos that show workers in action. There are sidebars and notes on ways to explore the field, related jobs, fun facts, profiles of people in the field, or lists of Web sites and books that might be helpful. At the end of the book you will find a glossary, which gives brief definitions of words that relate to education, career training, or employment that you may be unfamiliar with. There is an index of all the job titles mentioned in the book, followed by a list of math Web sites.

It's not too soon to think about your future. We hope you discover several possible career choices. Happy hunting!

Actuaries

What Actuaries Do

Actuaries are mathematicians who design and plan insurance and pension programs for businesses. They make mathematical calculations to help insurance companies figure out how much money they may have to pay to the businesses and workers they insure. They also figure out how much the policies should cost.

Insurance policies are formal agreements between insurance companies and policyholders. The policyholder pays a certain amount of money for the policy. This is usually a monthly fee called a *premium*. In return, the insurance company agrees to pay money to policyholders if they later suffer certain financial losses, such as those caused by accidents, illness, unemployment, or death. For example, if an insurance policyholder has a car accident, he or she files a claim with the insurance company. The claim shows the cost of the accident, including the cost to repair damage to the car or the amount of doctor bills to treat injuries. Insurance companies have created many different kinds of insurance; including life, medical, automobile, fire, and unemployment insurance. Many insurance companies also may handle pension programs. Pension is money paid to a worker after retirement.

Actuaries try to predict the number of policyholders who will have losses and how much money the insurance company will have to pay in claims. They then help the insurance company set prices for policies so that it always will have enough money to pay all the claims.

Actuaries use their knowledge of mathematics, probability, statistics, and principles of finance and business. Usually they begin by collecting and studying facts on events such as births, deaths, marriage, and employment. They then make tables to show the rates at which deaths, accidents, sickness, disability, or retirement occur. For example, when they set the cost for earthquake insurance, actuaries look at how often an earthquake happens in the homeowner's area. If the owner lives in California, the insurance is going to be more expensive than for someone

EXPLORING

If you think you are interested in becoming an actuary, try activities that allow you to practice strategy and problem solving skills. For example, you might join the school chess club, math club, or investment club. Participate in other activities that teach you leadership and management, such as student council positions.

1999 Jobs Rated Almanac Best Jobs

1. Web Site Manager

2. Actuary

3. Computer Systems Analyst

IT'S A FACT

• The term actuary was used for the first time in 1762 in the charter for the Equitable Society of London, the first life insurance company to use scientific data in figuring premiums. The basis of actuarial work started when French mathematicians Blaise Pascal (1623-62) and Pierre de Fermat (1601-65) figured out a way to calculate actuarial probabilities. Their work resulted in what is now called the science of probability.

• The first mortality table was produced when Edmund Halley (1656-1742) noticed that there were more male births than female births. He noticed that other such social events happened regularly. Halley, the English astronomer for whom Halley's Comet is named, is known as the father of life insurance.

• In 1889, a small group of actuaries formed the Actuarial Society of America. Two classes of members, fellows and associates, were created seven years later, and special examinations were developed to determine membership eligibility. Forms of these examinations are still used today. By 1909 the American Institute of Actuaries was created, and in 1949 these two groups joined into the present Society of Actuaries.

who lives in Kansas, because California has so many more earthquakes than Kansas does. But the tornado insurance for a Kansas home is more expensive than for a California home, because Kansas has a lot of tornadoes and California does not.

Education and Training

To be an actuary, you must like math and be able to do careful, detailed work. In high school you should take as much mathematics as possible. Computer science training is also important. After high school, you will have to go to college to earn a bachelor's degree. in mathematics or statistics.

Employers prefer to hire actuaries who have successfully passed a series of special examinations. The first two of these examinations should be taken while still in college. Actuaries usually take the other exams after they start working.

Earnings

College graduates who have passed one or two of the examinations begin making around $36,500 a year. College graduates who become actuaries without passing any of the examinations make salaries that average slightly less. Actuaries who complete all of the examinations make salaries that average $93,500 a year, Executives of insurance companies can make $100,000 a year or more.

Outlook

Because growth of the insurance industry has slowed recently, there will be fewer jobs for actuaries in the next ten years. Competition for entry-level jobs will be especially stiff.

FOR MORE INFO

American Academy of Actuaries
475 North Martingale Road, Suite 800
Schaumburg, IL 60173
Web: http://www.actuary.org

American Society of Pension Actuaries
4350 North Fairfax Drive, Suite 820
Arlington, VA 22203
Tel: 703-516-9300
Email: ASPA@aspa.org
Web: http://www.aspa.org

Society of Actuaries
475 North Martingale Road, Suite 800
Schaumburg, IL 60173
Tel: 847-706-3500
Web: http://www.soa.org

RELATED JOBS

Life Insurance Agents and Brokers

Mathematicians

Property and Casualty Insurance Agents and Brokers

Astronomers

NASA has a Web site especially for kids. You can learn about Earth and the other planets, space travel, the stars and galaxies, and NASA. You can even see a launch online. Here's the address: http://www.nasa.gov/kids.html

What Astronomers Do

Astronomers study the universe and all the celestial, or cosmic, bodies in space. They use telescopes, computers, and complex measuring tools to find the positions of stars and planets. They calculate the orbits of comets, asteroids, and artificial satellites. They study how celestial objects form and deteriorate, and they try to figure out how the universe started.

With special equipment, astronomers collect and analyze information about planets and stars, such as temperature, shape, size, brightness, and motion. They use this knowledge to help scientists know when to launch a space vehicle or a satellite. The astronomer's work also helps other scientists to better understand space, the origins of the earth and the universe, and the atmosphere surrounding the earth.

Because the field of astronomy is so broad, astronomers usually specialize in

Astronomers use telescopes to track changes in the sky and to search for new stars and galaxies.

one area of study. For example, *stellar astronomers* study the stars. *Solar astronomers* study the sun. *Planetary astronomers* study conditions on the planets. *Cosmologists* study the origin and the structure of the universe and astrophysicists study the physical and chemical changes that happen in the universe. *Celestial mechanics specialists* study the motion and position of planets and other objects in the solar system. *Radio astronomers* study the source and nature of celestial radio waves using sensitive radio telescopes.

Most astronomers teach at universities or colleges. A few lecture at planetariums and teach classes for the public. Some work at research institutions or at observatories. Those who work at observato-

EXPLORING

• Join an amateur astronomy club. There are many such clubs all over the country. These clubs usually have telescopes and will let members of the public view the night skies.
• Visit a nearby planetarium and ask astronomers who work there about their jobs. Planetariums also help you learn more about the universe and see if this is a career you would like.
• There are many astronomy sites on the Internet. Visit the National Aeronautics and Space Administration (NASA) Web site at http://www.nasa.gov for information on astronomy including links to other sites. Another site, *Astronomy Magazine*, will tell you when you might be able to see a comet or meteor shower. Look up http://www.kalmbach.com/astro/astronomy.html

WILL ASTEROIDS STRIKE EARTH?

Earth and all the other planets and moons have been continuously hit by asteroids and comets. Craters on the Moon are evidence of those strikes. Some people believe an asteroid or comet could strike the Earth and cause a disaster. But how likely is this? Astronomers and other scientists say such an event is not very likely. The most dangerous asteroids, those capable of causing major disasters, are extremely rare, according to NASA. These objects hit Earth once every 100,000 years on average.

ries spend three to six nights a month observing the night sky through a telescope. They spend the rest of their time in offices or laboratories where they study, analyze their data, and write reports. Other astronomers work for government agencies or private industry.

Education and Training

Training to become an astronomer can begin in high school. You should plan to take classes in mathematics, chemistry, physics, geography, and foreign languages (especially French, German, and Russian). Because astronomy is a high-technology field, you should try to learn as much as you can about computers.

After high school, you will have to earn a bachelor's degree in physics, mathematics, or astronomy. Once you receive your bachelor's degree, you may find work as an assistant or researcher. Most astronomers go on to earn both a master's degree and a doctorate.

Earnings

Professors at colleges or universities earn between $30,000 and $63,000 a year. Salaries for astronomers who work for the government are usually higher than for astronomers in teaching or observatory positions. The federal government employs astronomers at the National Aeronautics and Space Administration (NASA), the U.S. Naval Observatory, the Army Map Service, and the Naval Research Laboratory. The average salary of these astronomers is about $47,500 a year, according to a survey by the Commission on Professionals in Science and Technology.

Outlook

Astronomy is one of the smallest science fields, so people trained in astronomy must compete with many others for the best jobs. Many astronomers

FOR MORE INFO

For more information about a career in astronomy, contact the following:

American Astronomical Society
2000 Florida Avenue, Suite 400
Washington, DC 20009
Tel: 202-328-2010
Web: http://www.aas.org

American Institute of Physics
One Physics Ellipse
College Park, MD 20740-3843
Tel: 301-209-3100
Web: http://www.aip.org

Amateur Astronomers Association
1010 Park Avenue
New York, NY 10028
Tel: 212-535-2922
Web: http://www.aaa.org

find jobs in universities and government agencies. The Bureau of Labor Statistics says there will be fewer new jobs for astronomers in the government. The greatest growth in the field of astronomy will be in jobs in business and industry. These jobs may include helping a company that makes space equipment, for example.

Auditors

Bean Counters No More

Accountants and auditors have long been called bean counters. Their work has been considered boring and tedious. People used to associate them with death, taxes, and bad news. But that has changed. Accountants and auditors do much more than record financial information. Computers now count the "beans" while accountants and auditors analyze the results.

What Auditors Do

Auditors study the business and financial records of a company to make sure that they are correct and complete. They help the company prevent mistakes and follow the laws for company record keeping. After they examine the records, auditors give reports to the company managers and suggest ways to improve their record-keeping practices.

There are several kinds of auditors. *Internal auditors* are employees of a company. They help the company's accountants keep accurate records. They may also examine records to make sure employees are not using the company's money and property improperly.

Independent auditors work for a separate auditing company. Businesses hire them on a temporary basis to check their records and to make sure their own auditors and accountants are accurate. Independent auditors sometimes must travel to companies in other cities.

Tax auditors examine taxpayers' records to figure the correct amount of taxes they owe. Most tax auditors work for the state or federal government.

Education and Training

If you want to become an auditor, you must do well in math class, even in grade school. In high school, you should continue your math studies and also take classes in business, such as bookkeeping, and computer courses. Classes in English, speech, and writing, also are helpful.

To be an auditor, you must first study to become an accountant. You can find accountant training at business schools, junior colleges, colleges, and universities. You will need to earn a bachelor's degree with a major in accounting.

College graduates with two years of experience in internal auditing can take an exam offered by the Institute of Internal Auditors. When you pass this exam you become a Certified Internal Auditor. After college, you will have to take more classes and pass an examination to become a Certified Public Accountant (CPA). In

EXPLORING

• You can get experience in accounting and auditing skills by volunteering to be treasurer for school clubs or organizations.

• If your school has a fund-raising event, you could offer to keep track of the financial records.

• Ask your parents to show you how to balance a checkbook.

• Keep a spending diary. Write down what you buy each day and how much it costs. How much have you saved?

IT'S A FACT

- Accounting records and bookkeeping methods have been used since ancient times. Records discovered in Babylonia (modern-day Iraq) date back to 3600 BC. Accounts were kept by the ancient Greeks and the Romans.

- Modern accounting began with double-entry bookkeeping, which was developed by Luca Pacioli (c.1450-c.1520), an Italian mathematician.

- The accounting profession in the United States dates back only to 1880, when English and Scottish investors began to buy stock in American companies. To keep an eye on their investments, they sent over accountants. When the accountants saw the great opportunities in the accounting field, they stayed in America to establish their own businesses.

- The government started to collect income tax in 1913.

most states, large public accounting firms hire only CPAs.

Earnings

Auditors earn average salaries of $35,000 a year. They start at about $25,000. Auditors' salaries vary according to their experience, the type of business that employs them, and the difficulty of the accounting systems they are auditing. More experienced auditors may earn $50,000 or more a year. Auditors who work for the federal government earn less than those in private industry.

Outlook

The need for auditors is expected to grow because businesses' accounting needs are continuing to expand. Managers rely heavily on accounting information to make business decisions.

FOR MORE INFO

For more information about certification and a career as an auditor, contact:
Institute of Internal Auditors
249 Maitland Avenue
Altamont Springs, FL 32701-4201
Tel: 407-830-7600
Email: iia@theiia.org
Web: http://www.theiia.org

For information about the Uniform CPA Examination and about becoming a Student Affiliate Member, contact:
American Institute of Certified Public Accountants
1211 Avenue of the Americas
New York, NY 10036-8775
Tel: 212-596-6200
Web: http://www.aicpa.org

For information on certification, contact::
The Information Systems Audit and Control Association
3701 Algonquin Road, Sulte 1010
Rolling Meadows, IL 60008
Tel: 847-253-1545
Web: http://www.isaca.org

RELATED JOBS

Accountants
Bookkeepers
Cashiers
Tax Preparers

Bank Services Occupations

In 1970, the country's first automatic teller machine was installed at Citizens and Southern National Bank in Valdosta, Georgia.

RELATED JOBS

Accountants
Auditors
Bookkeepers
Business Managers
Cashiers
Clerks
Management Analysts and Consultants

What Bank Services Workers Do

A bank receives, exchanges, lends, and safeguards money. Changes in the economy and the increasing use of computers and automatic teller machines affect the banking industry and the many people who work there.

Bank tellers handle certain types of customer account transactions. These employees serve the public directly. They accept customers' deposits and give them receipts. They also pay out withdrawals, record transactions, and cash checks. In addition, they make sure that there is enough money in the account to cover the check.

Bank clerks help to keep the vast amounts of paperwork and the computerized records in a bank in order. They keep track of deposit slips, checks, financial statements, and correspondence.

They record transactions and file records. They may assist customers, answer telephone calls, and do other general duties.

Bank officers and managers supervise workers and handle loans and other financial matters at a bank. They are responsible for directing employees, making assignments, and overseeing day-to-day operations. Bank officers might also work in accounting, public relations, advertising, or other areas of a bank. Officers review budgets and other financial records. A manager or officer must research what other local banks are doing and how strong the economy is. These factors will influence what services the bank's customers will want. The bank officer usually prepares daily or weekly reports for the bank president.

Education and Training

Most banks prefer that bank clerks and bank tellers have completed high school. Employers look for applicants who have taken courses in bookkeeping, typing, business, and mathematics. You should also be able to operate business machines.

Bank officers and managers need to understand finances, economics, and the

EXPLORING

• Volunteer to be the banker when you play games like Monopoly.

• Ask your parents to teach you how to write checks and how to use a checkbook.

• Ask your parents to help you open your own bank account.

• Visit these Web sites:

Moneycents
http://www.kidsmoneycents.com

Kids' Money Store
http://www.kidsmoneystore.com/

A BIT OF BANKING HISTORY

Banking in the United States began right after the Revolutionary War. The First Bank of the United States was a federal bank established to print money, purchase securities (stocks and bonds) in companies, and lend money. It was also responsible for setting lending rules that state banks would have to follow. At the end of its 20-year charter, Congress refused to renew the First Bank's charter because of concern about the power that the bank held. The bank was soon closed.

Another federal bank followed but only operated for four years before it suffered the same fate as the First Bank. With the failures of the federal banks, state banks quickly grew in power and size. Each bank was allowed to issue its own currency, which created a huge variation in the number of dollars actually in existence. This, in turn, affected the value of each dollar.

If the bank produced too much money, or lent money and did not receive enough of it back, the bank would close and depositors would lose everything they had invested. This was a continual problem throughout the 1800s, but particularly from 1800 to 1863. This era was known as the Wildcat Period.

In 1863-64, The National Banks Act was passed to charter state banks, issue national currency, and eventually tax the usage of bank currency. The taxation effectively killed all but the national currency.

In 1913 Congress established the Federal Reserve. In response to a series of financial panics set off by the limited number of dollars being printed, the Federal Reserve was started to act as the government's central bank. It was divided into 12 districts, with a board of governors to determine policy, supervise the fluctuation of currency reserves for banks, and print currency.

What It Takes

To be a bank worker you must:
• Be outgoing and friendly.
• Be able to handle the occasional irate customer.
• Be honest and accurate.
• Pay close attention to detail.
• Have a solid understanding of financial matters.

rules and regulations of the banking industry. To become a bank officer or manager you will need a bachelor's degree in economics or business administration.

Earnings

Bank tellers earn average salaries of $16,300 a year. Clerks' salaries range from $19,300 to $24,700. After several years of experience, they earn $23,000 to $37,000 a year. Bank officers and managers have starting salaries of $21,800. Experienced officers and managers earn $81,100 or more a year.

Outlook

Employment opportunities are expected to decline for bank tellers because more people use automatic teller machines and online banking. The outlook is better for bank clerks and related workers. As urban areas expand, many banks are opening branch operations. Clerks will be needed in these new facilities. Faster than aver-

FOR MORE INFO

For more information, contact the following organizations:
American Bankers Association
1120 Connecticut Avenue, NW
Washington, DC 20036
Tel: 800-338-0626
Web: http://www.aba.com/aba

Bank Administration Institute
One North Franklin Street, Suite 1000
Chicago, IL 60606-3421
Tel: 800-224-9889
Email: info@bai.org
Web: http://www.bai.org

Institute of Financial Education
55 West Monroe, Suite 2800
Chicago, IL 60601-4680
Tel: 312-946-0488
Web: http://www.theinstitute.com

age growth is predicted for bank officers and managers. They will be needed to face greater competition, to handle changing tax laws, and to help banks comply with stricter record keeping policies.

Bookkeepers

What Bookkeepers Do

Bookkeepers keep records of the finances of their companies. They may record these transactions in an account book or in a computer. From time to time, they prepare statements that summarize the funds received and paid out.

Bookkeeping records are very important to any company. They show how much money the company has and how much it owes. They also show how much money the company has earned or lost in a certain period of time. Bookkeeping records are especially important when a company submits income tax reports to the federal government and profit and loss reports to company owners.

Bookkeepers work for a wide variety of employers. These range from small businesses to large corporations. For example, bookkeepers may work for factories, stores, schools, banks, insurance companies, hotels, or railroads. *General book-*

keepers usually work for small businesses. They may do all the tasks involved in keeping a complete set of bookkeeping records. They use adding machines, calculators, and computers. They may also do other types of office work, such as filing papers and answering telephone calls.

In large businesses, an accountant may supervise the workers in the bookkeeping department. These workers sometimes are called *accounting clerks.* They usually do specialized tasks. Some record items in account books and make out bills. Others prepare reports, write checks, or make payroll lists.

Bookkeepers need strong mathematical skills. They must be organized and able to concentrate on detailed work. The work is often tedious, and bookkeepers should not mind sitting for long hours behind a desk. They should be methodical, accurate, and orderly and enjoy working on detailed tasks. Employers look for honest, discreet, and trustworthy people, because they are placing their business in the bookkeeper's hands.

EXPLORING

• Keep an account of your own finances. Write down your income, including your allowance, gifts, or money you earn for odd jobs or babysitting. Write down your expenses—food and drink, clothing, music and movies, etc.

• Volunteer to be the treasurer for school clubs.

• Use your school's resource center or local library to find computer software designed for money management.

WHERE IT ALL BEGAN

Bookkeeping developed along with the growth of business and industry. The first known records of bookkeeping date back to 2600 BC, when the Babylonians used pointed sticks to mark accounts on clay slabs. By 3000 BC, Middle Eastern and Egyptian cultures used a system of numbers to record merchants' trading of the grain and farm products that were distributed from storage warehouses.

Sometime after the start of the 13th century, the decimal numeration system was introduced in Europe, simplifying bookkeeping record systems. The merchants of Venice—one of the busiest trading centers in the world at that time—are credited with the invention of the double entry bookkeeping method that is widely used today.

As industry in the United States expands and grows more complex, simpler and quicker bookkeeping methods and procedures have evolved. Technological developments include bookkeeping machines, computer hardware and software, and electronic data-processing.

Education and Training

Bookkeepers must have at lea[st] a high school education. Employers prefer to hire those who have taken business cour[s]es in high school. Such course[s] include business, math, book-keeping, and computers. Som[e] employers look for people wh[o] have completed a junior colle[ge]

Bookkeeping Equipment

Fax machine

Copier

Computer with spreadsheet, word processing, and database software

Adding machine

Reference books, such as a yearly tax guide

or business school training program. Others offer on-the-job training to workers.

Some schools and employers participate in work-study programs. In these programs, students work at part-time bookkeeping jobs. They also are required to attend class and complete class assignments.

FOR MORE INFO

For more information about a career as a bookkeeper, contact:
Foundation for Accounting Education
530 Fifth Avenue, 5th Floor
New York, NY 10036-5101
Tel: 800-537-3635

Earnings

Beginning accounting clerks in private business make an average of $20,700 a year. Experienced bookkeepers average $24,000 a year. Top paying jobs average about $30,000 a year.

Outlook

More than 2.2 million people work in bookkeeping jobs. However, employment of bookkeepers and accounting clerks is expected to decline in the next ten years. Most job openings will only be created as workers retire or change jobs. New jobs will become available as smaller businesses and industries expand. The use of computers makes the bookkeeper's job easier, but it also means that businesses need fewer bookkeepers to do the same amount of work. Nearly all new positions for bookkeepers will be created in small, rapidly growing organizations.

RELATED JOBS

Accountants
Auditors
Bank Services Workers
Clerks
Tax Preparers

Computer Programmers

Computer Programmer Sees the Future

CNN reports that a Michigan computer programmer, Bill Schoen, foresaw the Y2K bug coming 16 years before the turn of the century. He says says he lost his job because no one believed that there would be any problems when the years rolled from 1999 to 2000.

What Computer Programmers Do

Computer programmers write and code the instructions for computers. Computers operate by following these carefully prepared instructions.

Computer programmers work for companies that create and sell computer hardware and software. They also work for all kinds of businesses, from manufacturers of office machines to distributors of machinery and equipment. They work for banks, hospitals, schools, and the federal government.

To do their work, programmers have to break down each step of a task into a series of instructions that the computer can understand. Then programmers translate the instructions into a specific computer language. COBOL and FORTRAN are the names of two computer languages. Then programmers test the program to make sure it works. They cor-

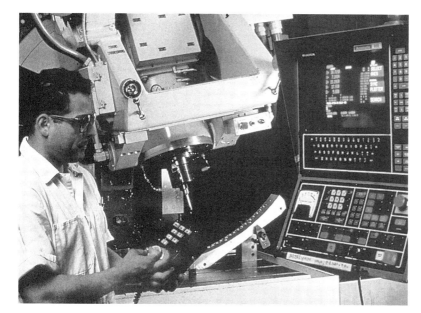

Numerical control tool programmers write computer programs that operate machine tools in the manufacturing industry.

rcct any errors. This is called debugging the program. Finally, they write the instructions for the operators who will use the program. Some programs can be created in a few hours. Others may take more than a year of work. Programmers often work together on teams for a large project.

There are two basic kinds of computer programmers: *systems programmers* and *applications programmers.* Systems programmers must understand and care for an entire computer system, including its software, its memory, and all of its related equipment, such as terminals, printers, and disk drives. Applications programmers write the programs that do particular tasks—word processing, account-

EXPLORING

• The best way to learn about computers is to use one—either at home surfing the Internet or at school.
• Join a computer club and find others who are interested in computers and programming.
• It is a good idea to start early and get some hands-on experience operating and programming a computer.
• You will find countless books on programming at your local library or bookstore. There are plenty of resources to teach yourself no matter how much experience you have.

COMPUTERS ARRIVE ON THE SCENE

Data processing systems developed during World War II. The amount of information that had to be collected and organized for war efforts became so great that it was not possible for people to prepare it in time to make decisions. A quicker way had to be invented.

After the war, the new computer technology was put to use in other government operations as well as in businesses. The first computer used by civilians was installed by the Bureau of the Census in 1951 to help gather data from the 1950 census. At this time, computers were large, cumbersome, and energy-draining. Three years later, the first computer was installed by a business firm. Today, computers are used in government agencies, industrial firms, banks, insurance agencies, schools, publishing companies, scientific laboratories, and homes.

ing, databases, and games. They usually specialize in a field, such as business, engineering, or science. Systems programmers often help applications programmers with complicated tasks.

Education and Training

Most employers prefer to hire college graduates. There are many colleges that offer courses and degree programs in computer science.. A number of two-year programs in data processing, and junior-level programming are available in junior and community colleges. Some employers may want their programmers to be trained in their specific area. For example, a computer programmer for an engineering firm might need an engineering degree. Most employers look for candidates who are patient, persistent, very logical in their thinking, and who can work under pressure without making mistakes. Because programmers work in so many different industries, there is no standard way to begin as a computer programmer. After you learn the basics of computer programming, you should choose a field that interests you and then look for programming opportunities in that field. It can take up to a year to master all aspects of a programming job. Opportunities for advancement are great.

Earnings

The average earnings for full-time programmers are about $40,100 a year. Some programmers earn more than $65,200 a year. Beginning positions pay about $35,000 a year in private business and $19,500 a year in government.

Outlook

As we continue to rely more and more on computers to store and analyze data, employment opportunities for comput-

FOR MORE INFO

For more information, contact the following organizations:
Association for Computing Machinery
One Astor Plaza
1515 Broadway
New York, NY 10036
Tel: 212-869-7440
Email: ACMHELP@acm.org
Web: http://www.acm.org

Association of Information Technology Professionals
315 South Northwest Highway, Suite 200
Park Ridge, IL 60068-4278
Tel: 800-224-9371
Web: http://www.aitp/org

er programmers should also continue to grow through 2006. The best jobs will go to college graduates who know several programming languages and who are trained in a specific field, such as accounting, science, engineering, or management.

Computer Systems Analysts

Where Do They Work?

Computer systems/programmer analysts work for all types of firms, like these:

Manufacturing companies

Data processing service firms

Hardware and software companies

Banks

Insurance companies

Credit companies

Publishing companies

Government agencies

Colleges and universities

What Computer Systems Analysts Do

Computer systems analysts help banks, government offices, and businesses understand their computer systems. Most offices now use computers to store data. They need analysts who can design computer systems and programs for the specific needs of a business, or even to the needs of just one department in a business.

Computer systems analysts work with both the hardware and software parts of computer systems. The hardware includes the large items such as the computer itself, the monitor, and the keyboard. The software includes the computer programs, which are written and stored on disks, and the documentation (the manuals or guidebooks) that goes with the programs. Analysts design the best mix of hardware and software for the needs of the company that employs them.

A computer systems analyst for the per-

EXPLORING

• Play strategy games, such as chess. Such games are a good way to use analytic thinking skills while having fun. Commercial games range in themes from war simulations to world historical development.

• Learn everything you can about computers. Work and play with them on a daily basis. Surf the Internet regularly and read computer magazines. You might want to try hooking up a mini-system at home or school, configuring terminals, printers, and modems. This activity requires a fair amount of knowledge and should be supervised by a professional.

sonnel department of a large company, for example, would first talk to the department manager about which areas of the business could be helped by computer technology. The company started a new policy of giving employees longer paid vacations at Christmas. The manager might want to know how this policy has affected company profits for the month of December. The analyst can show the manager what computer program to use, what data to enter, and how to read the charts or graphs that the computer produces. The work of the analyst allows the manager to review the raw data. In this case, the numbers show that company profits were the same as in the previous Decembers. The manager can then decide whether to continue the company policy.

Once analysts have the computer system set up and operating, they advise on equipment and programming changes. Often, two or more people in a department each have their own computer, but they must be able to connect with and use information from each other's computers. Analysts must then work with all the different computers in a department or a company so the computers can connect with each other. This system of connected computers is called a network.

Education and Training

To be a computer systems analyst you will need at least a bachelor's degree in computer science. Analysts in specialized areas (aeronautics, for example) usually have graduate degrees as well. Also, training in mathematics, engineering, account-

ing, or business will be helpful in some cases.

In addition to a college degree, job experience as a computer programmer is very helpful. Many businesses choose computer programmers already on

IT'S A FACT

• More than 50 percent of all systems analysts work in the Midwest or Northeast.

• About 482,900 people worked in this occupation in 1994.

• Only 5 percent of systems analysts work part-time.

• About 31 percent of systems analysts are women.

• The unemployment rate for systems analysts was 2.2 percent in the period from 1994 to 1996. The average for all occupations was 6.7 percent.

staff and train them on the job to be systems analysts. Computer systems analysts with several years of experience are often promoted into managerial jobs.

Although it is not required, computer systems analysts can become certified by the Institute for Certification of Computer Professionals. Analysts take classes and exams to become a Certified Systems Professional (CSP). This certification may help you get a job.

FOR MORE INFO

For more information about the career of computer system analyst, contact the following organizations:

Association for Systems Management
1433 West Bagley Road
PO Box 38370
Cleveland, OH 44138
Tel: 216-234-2930

Institute for Certification of Computing Professionals
2200 East Devon Avenue, Suite 246
Des Plaines, IL 60018
Tel: 800-843-8422
Web: http://www.iccp.org

Earnings

Starting salaries for computer systems analysts average about $46,300 a year. After several years of experience, analysts can earn as much as $59,000 a year. Computer systems analysts with many years of experience and a master's degree can earn salaries of $63,000 a year and higher. Salaries for analysts in government are somewhat lower than the average for private industry. Earnings also depend on years of experience and the type of business you work for.

Outlook

This field is one of the fastest growing careers. Companies are always looking for qualified analysts, especially those with advanced degrees in computer science.

Demographers

What Demographers Do

Demographers collect and study facts about their society's population—births, marriages, deaths, education, and income levels. Their population studies tell what the society is really like and help experts forecast economic and social trends. For example, demographers may study birth rates of a community. They may find that the population of school-age children is growing faster than expected and that new schools will have to be built. Or demographers may collect facts about how many of these children have been sick with measles. These facts could be studied to find out how effective the measles vaccine is.

Demographers work for both government agencies and private companies. Local, state, and federal government agencies use demographers to help them provide enough of the right kinds of transportation, education, police, and health services. Private companies need demogra-

Why Do We Need Population Statistics?

Population statistics, the basic tool of demography, include total population figures, population density (the average number of persons inhabiting each square mile), age, sex, and racial groupings, among other data.

Population statistics are used as the basis for assigning seats in the House of Representatives among the states. For example, New York would receive more seats than Montana because there are more people per square mile. Accurate population statistics are necessary in planning immigration policies, public health programs, advertising and marketing campaigns, and other activities.

phers' collections of facts, or statistics, to help them improve their products or services and know who will buy them. For example, a retail chain might use a demographer's study to help decide the best location to open a new store. Demographers may also teach in colleges and universities or work as consultants for private companies or communities as a whole.

Demographers use computers to help them gather and analyze the millions of pieces of information they need to make their forecasts. It is up to the individual demographer to know how to read the statistics and put them together in a meaningful way.

Education and Training

Students interested in this field should be good at solving logical problems and have strong skills in numbers and mathematics, especially algebra and geometry. In high school, you should take classes in social studies, English and mathematics. Training in computer science also is helpful.

Demographers need a college degree in sociology or public health with special studies in demography. Many entry-level jobs require a master's degree.

EXPLORING

Visit these Web sites to learn more about demography, statistics, and census information:

The Fedstat Search Engine
http://www.fedstats.gov/search.html

U.S. Bureau of the Census
http://www.census.gov

Macro International
http://www.macroint.com

Johns Hopkins Center for Communications Programs
http://www.jhuccp.org/netlinks

The CIA World Fact Book
http://www.odci.gov/cia/publicaitons/factbook/index.html

Also see For More Information on page 37.

As the field gets more competitive, many demographers (especially those who wish to work for the federal government) will earn a doctorate in sociology. The most successful demographers specialize in one area. You must also keep up with advances in the field by continuing education throughout your career.

Earnings

Earnings vary according to education, training, and place of employment. Social scientists (including sociologists who specialize in demography) with a bachelor's degree receive starting salaries averaging around $25,000 a year. Those in federal government positions with no experience might start around

$19,500 a year. Demographers with master's degrees start at about $29,600 a year. Those with Ph.D. degrees start at $35,800 a year.

Outlook

There is a large amount of fact-gathering and social science research going on in the United States. The need for trained demographers to analyze this research should grow a little more slowly than the average through the year 2006. Job opportunities will be greatest in and around large cities, because that is where many colleges, universities, and other research facilities are located. There may be an increasing demand for demographers in international organizations such as the World Bank, the United Nations, and the World Health Organization. Demographers in these organizations will be needed to help developing countries analyze their own growing populations and plan for necessary services.

FOR MORE INFO

ASA offers many free career publications, lists of accredited schools, and college student membership, as well as job information.
American Sociological Association
1307 New York Avenue, NW, Suite 700
Washington, DC 20005
Tel: 202-383-9005
Email: executive.office@asa.net.org
Web: http://www.asanet.org

For information about the U.S. Census Bureau including a list of regional offices, jobs, and a calendar of events, contact:
Census Bureau
Public Information Office
Department of Commerce
Jacob K. Javitz Federal Building
Room 37-130
New York, NY 10278
Tel: 212-264-3860
Web: http://www.census.org

This organization publishes a magazine and a newsletter, holds workshops and discussion groups, and lists job opportunities.
Population Association of America
1875 Connecticut Ave., NW, Suite 520
Washington, DC 20009
Tel: 202-483-5158
Business Office
721 Ellsworth Dr., Suite 303
Silver Spring, MD 20910
Tel: 301-565-6710
Email: 74761.1510@compuserve.com
Web: http://www.popassoc.org

Engineers

Engineering Specialties

Aerospace Engineers
Air Quality Engineers
Biomedical Engineers
Ceramics Engineers
Chemical Engineers
Civil Engineers
Electrical and
Electronics Engineers
Environmental
Engineers
Hardware Engineers
Industrial Engineers
Mechanical Engineers
Metallurgical Engineers
Mining Engineers
Nuclear Engineers
Optical Engineers
Packaging Engineers
Petroleum Engineers
Plastics Engineers
Software Engineers
Traffic Engineers

What Engineers Do

Engineers, more than any other professionals, are responsible for discoveries and inventions that are part of our everyday lives. They use scientific knowledge and tools to design products, structures, and machines. Most engineers specialize in a particular area. *Electrical and electronic engineers,* for example, work in the medical, computer, missile guidance, and power distribution fields. Engineers have a wide range of choices in the type of work they want to do. Almost every industry uses some type of engineer.

A nuclear power station is a good example of how different engineering specialties work together. *Civil engineers* help select the site for the power station. They draw blueprints for all structural details of the building. *Nuclear engineers* handle every stage of the production of nuclear energy, from processing nuclear fuels to the disposal of radioactive wastes. *Environmental engineers* also find ways

to safely dispose of such wastes. *Mechanical engineers* design and build engines that use nuclear fuel to produce power. *Electrical engineers* design equipment to distribute the electricity to thousands of customers. The device workers wear to detect the levels of radiation their bodies absorb over a period of time was developed by *biomedical engineers.*

There are 1.4 million engineers in the United States. All engineers, whatever their specialty, have a strong math and science background and an ability to develop solutions to practical problems. All engineers are problem solvers and inventors. They all do highly technical work. They must have a thorough knowledge of how things work, from electronics to the human body, in order to come

EXPLORING

• Join science and math clubs at your school.

• Work on science projects that involve inventing and building. Enter a project in a science fair.

• Ask your librarian to help you find books on engineering, such as these:
Adams, James L. *Flying Buttresses, Entropy, and O-Rings: The World of an Engineer* (Harvard University Press, 1993).

Norman, Donald A. *The Design of Everyday Things* (Doubleday, 1990).

"Although women earn 29 percent of bachelor's of science degrees in science and engineering, only 18 percent of all employed engineers and scientists are women. What's this about? Many women shy away from careers like engineering or medicine because they don't think they will succeed there. Like a fish out of water, many women feel like they just won't survive."

Breaking Free: Women in Nontraditional Careers. *Teen Voices* Volume 8, Issue 3, pp. 44-47.

mechanical, or civil engineering. Graduates of these programs may then choose to further specialize in their area of interest by taking more college courses or getting on-the-job training. For example, a mechanical engineer who wants to work with nuclear reactors may study nuclear science beyond the undergraduate level or may take an entry-level engineering job at a nuclear plant before working up to becoming an actual nuclear engineer.

up with better ways of doing things.

Education and Training

Engineers all have at least a four-year degree that gives them a clear understanding of how math and science applies to the everyday world. Most engineering degrees are in electrical,

Much of the work engineers do affects the safety of the public. For this reason, engineers usually must be licensed in the states where they work. All 50 states require registration for engineers whose work may affect life, health, or property, or who offer their services to the public. To be registered, engineers must have an undergraduate degree, four years of professional experience, and successful completion of a state examination.

Earnings

Engineers are paid well for their work. Their salaries are among the highest starting salaries of any career. New engineers with bachelor's degrees average $38,500 a year. Those with master's degrees and no experience earn an average of $45,400 a year. Engineers with several years of experience and education can earn $100,000 or more a year.

Outlook

Engineers have great job security. Their work is necessary for keeping and improving our way of life. Even when the economy is not healthy, engineers' jobs are generally safe. Demand will continue to be strong for engineers with a solid math and science background and training in new technologies.

FOR MORE INFO

For more information on careers, education, special programs, and student memberships, contact:

American Society for Engineering Education
1818 N Street, NW, Suite 600
Washington, DC 20036
Tel: 202-331-3500
Web: http://www.asee.org

Junior Engineering Technical Society, Inc.
1420 King Street, Suite 405
Alexandria, VA 22314-2794
Tel: 703-548-5387
Web: http://www.jets.org/jets

National Society of Professional Engineers
1420 King Street
Alexandria, VA 22314
Tel: 703-684-2800
Web: http://www.nspe.org

RELATED JOBS

Mathematicians
Operatioins Research Analysts
Physicists

Financial Planners

What Financial Planners Do

Financial planners advise their clients on many aspects of finance. They do not work alone. Financial planners meet with their clients' other advisors, such as attorneys, accountants, trust officers, and investment bankers. This helps financial planners understand everything about their clients' overall finances. After meeting with the clients and their other advisors, financial planners analyze the information and write a report. This report lists the clients' financial objectives, current income, investments, expenses, tax returns, insurance, retirement programs, estate plans, and other important information. The report also includes recommendations on how the clients can best achieve their financial goals.

Financial planning is an ongoing process. The plan must be reviewed often so that changes can be made, if necessary, to make sure that it continues to meet the client's needs.

Since they handle all of the money and investments that people have worked a lifetime to earn, financial planners must be ready to answer difficult questions about the plans they write.

People need financial planners for different things. Some might want life insurance, college savings plans, or estate planning. Sometimes these needs are caused by changes in people's lives, such as retirement, death of a spouse, disability, marriage, birth of children, or job changes. Financial planners spend most of their time on investment planning, retirement planning, tax planning, estate planning, and risk management. All of these areas require different types of financial knowledge.

For example, financial planners who are *retirement counselors* look at whether the client will be happy with simple living, or want to travel the world first class. Other issues must be addressed, such as relocation costs, if any, or medical insurance needs. They must know about traditional sources of retirement funds, such as Social Security, personal savings, employer-sponsored plans, post-retirement employment, and inheritance. Another

EXPLORING

• If you live near a stock exchange, go for a visit. Most exchanges have their own Web sites.

• Visit these Web sites:
Investing for Kids
http://library.thinkquest.org/3096/

The Monetta Express
http://www.monetta.com/kids/

The Young Investor
http://www.younginvestor.com/pick.html

U.S. Treasury's Page for Kids
http://www.treas.gov/kids/

retirement issue is the possibility of disability and the need for chronic illness care. Retirement planners may suggest disability income insurance, long-term care insurance, or a medical savings account as a precaution for such situations.

Planners must also know about asset management, employee benefits, insurance, and investments. Financial planners must have good people skills, since it is important to have good relationships with clients.

Financial planners use various ways to find new clients, such as telephone calls and giving seminars on financial planning.

Education and Training

In high school, you should take as many business classes as possible, as well as mathematics. Communications courses, such as speech or acting, help put you at ease with talking in front of a crowd. English courses will help you prepare written reports.

Most financial planners earn a bachelor's degree in business or science. You could earn a business administration degree with a specialty in financial planning. You could also earn a liberal

GLOSSARY

Assets: Resources that have money value, including cash, inventory, real estate, machinery, collectibles, and securities. **Current assets** are those that can be converted to cash within a year. A **fixed asset** is a long-term asset, such as a building, piece of land, or patent that will not be converted to cash within a year.

Liabilities: Debts or money owed. **Current liabilities** are debts that must be paid within a year.

Net income: Profit after taxes.

Net worth: Value found by subtracting all liabilities from all assets.

arts degree with courses in accounting, business administration, economics, finance, marketing, human behavior, counseling, and public speaking.

It is not required, but many financial planners become licensed as Certified Financial Planners (CFP) by the Certified Financial Board of the Institute of Certified Financial Planners. To become licensed, you must pass tests, have a certain amount of experience, and complete certain courses.

Earnings

The salary range for financial planners is $50,000 to $200,000 a year or more. The average hourly fee for financial planners is $100.

Outlook

Employment of financial planners is expected to grow rapidly in the future. The economy is good and people are earning more and inheriting more. This

FOR MORE INFO

For information on financial planning and certification, contact:
Certified Financial Planner Board of Standards
1700 Broadway, Suite 2100
Denver, CO 80290-2101
Tel: 303-830-7500
Web: http://www.cfp-board.org

Institute of Certified Financial Planners
3801 East Florida Avenue, Suite 708
Denver, CO 80210-2544
Tel: 303-759-4900
Web: http://www.icfp.org

means they will have more money to invest. More and more people will need advice from financial planners about the many investment choices available.

RELATED JOBS

Accountants
Financial Services Brokers
Retirement Counselors
Tax Preparers

Geophysicists

What Geophysicists Do

Geophysicists study the physical structure of the earth. This includes land surfaces, underground areas, and bodies of water. They use their knowledge to predict earthquakes, discover oil, and find places to build power plants. Their duties may include fieldwork, laboratory research, or college teaching.

Geophysics combines the sciences of geology and physics. Geophysicists usually specialize in one area of geophysics. For example, *seismologists* study earthquakes. *Hydrologists* study the movement and distribution of water. *Meteorologists* study weather patterns. No matter what their area of specialization, geophysicists use the scientific principles of geology, chemistry, mathematics, physics, and engineering. Many of their instruments, such as the seismograph, take precise measurements of the earth's physical characteristics, such as its electric, magnetic, and gravitational fields.

A geophysicist measures seismic activity on a fault.

Geophysicists often study environmental issues. For example, they may investigate whether an explosion designed to expose rich mineral deposits might also lead to an earthquake. They might examine the quality of underground water and how it affects a city's drinking supply.

Field geophysicists work outdoors in all kinds of weather. They often travel and work in isolated areas.

Education and Training

Geophysicists should have a solid background in mathematics and the physical and earth sciences. In high school you should take four years of mathematics

EXPLORING

• You can find out more about geophysics by reading books on electricity, rocks and minerals, metals and metallurgy, the universe and space, and weather and climate.

• Develop hobbies that deal with radio, electronics, rock collecting, or map collecting.

• Take a look at the Society of Exploration Geophysicists kids' Web site at http://students.seg.org/kids/

EARTHSHATTERING FACTS

• Scientists believe that the San Andreas fault may be one hundred million years old. It cuts through the state of California for almost 700 miles. Small earthquakes along the San Andreas fault occur several times a month. Not all earthquakes are dangerous, but many lives have been lost due to earthquakes along the fault. In the 1906 San Francisco earthquake, 500 people died from falling buildings and fires. The city burned for three days.

• There are over a million quakes around the world each year, including those too small to be felt.

• The most people killed in an earthquake is approximately 830,000 in China in 1556.

• The great Alaska earthquake of March 27, 1964, was the strongest earthquake in the United States. It had a magnitude of 9.2. Approximately 115 people died, with most of the deaths due to the tsunami (seismic wave) it generated. Shaking was felt for an estimated 7 minutes, and raised or lowered the ground surface as much as 56 feet in some areas.

• A magnitude 9.5 earthquake in Chile in 1960 was the largest known earthquake and resulted in over 6,000 deaths. It triggered a tsunami that killed people as far away as Hawaii and Japan.

• Alaska has more earthquakes per year than the combined total of the rest of the United States. As many as 4,000 are recorded there every year.

Source: Center for Earthquake Research and Information

and courses in earth science, physics, and chemistry. Classes in mechanical drawing, history, and English are also highly recommended.

The best way to become a geophysicist is to get a bachelor's degree in geophysics or geology. A degree in physics, mathematics, or chemistry might be sufficient, but you should also take as many geology courses as you can. You will need a master's degree or doctorate in geology or geophysics for research or college teaching positions, and other positions with good advancement potential.

Earnings

The average starting salary for a geophysicist is $30,900 a year. The average mid-range salary is $59,700. Experienced geophysicists with doctorates earn $90,000 a year.

Outlook

Many geophysicists explore for oil and gas. Their employment

For more information about a career as a geophysicist, contact:
American Geophysical Union
2000 Florida Avenue, NW
Washington, DC 20009
Tel: 202-462-6900
Web: http://www.agu.org

Society of Exploration Geophysicists
PO Box 702740
Tulsa, OK 74170-2740
Tel: 918-497-5500
Web: http://seg.org

opportunities depend on the strength of the petroleum industry. But even if job prospects in the oil industry are not good, there will continue to be jobs in teaching and other research areas.

Chemists
Geologists
Mining Engineers
Petrologists
Physicists

Math Teachers

What Math Teachers Do

Math teachers help students learn simple and advanced math theories and apply these concepts to everyday life.

Math teachers work in elementary, middle and high school classrooms. Some math teachers may also work as adult education teachers. Professors usually teach at the college level.

Math teachers teach complex mathematical subjects such as algebra, calculus, geometry, trigonometry, and statistics to middle and high school students. They may teach algebra to a class of ninth graders one period and trigonometry to high school seniors the next. Teachers must be able to get along with young people, have patience, and like to help others. They need good communication skills, since they often work with students from varying ethnic backgrounds and cultures.

A math teacher explains a theory to his students

Math teachers not only teach specific subjects, but they must make learning fun and teach students how to work together. Some schools use less structured classrooms to teach math skills, team problem solving, and cooperation. Math teachers encourage creative and logical thinking as it relates to math and education in general. They often use various teaching methods to keep students interested and help them learn. They may use games, computers, and experiments as hands-on teaching tools in the classroom. They may schedule field trips, guest speakers, or special events to show students how math skills are used in their daily lives and in the operation of businesses and government.

EXPLORING

• Teach a younger sister or brother to count or do basic arithmetic, such as addition and subtraction. As they get a little older, you can teach them the value of coins and how to make change.

• Your school or community may have a volunteer program where you can tutor younger children in math.

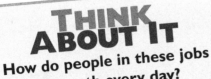

Carpentry

Cooking

Farming

Graphic design

Photography

Publishing

Real Estate

Sales

Sewing

Math teachers also develop lesson plans, create exams, correct papers, calculate grades, and keep records. Some schools may also require teachers to lead extracurricular activities such as math club, competitions, and events. Teachers meet with and advise students, hold parent/teacher conferences, and attend faculty meetings. In addition, they may have to attend local, state, and national conferences. Teachers must take continuing education courses to maintain their state's teaching license.

Education and Training

If you want to pursue a career as a math teacher, you should take high school math courses including algebra, geometry, trigonometry, and calculus. More advanced classes such as probability, statistics, and logic are also beneficial if they are available. Computer science, psychology, and English classes are also recommended.

Public school teachers in the United States and in the District of Columbia must be licensed. The state's board of education or a licensing committee usually grants this license. Although requirements for teaching licenses vary by state, all public schools require teachers to have a bachelor's degree and complete the state's approved training program.

Earnings

According to a 1997 report from the National Education Association (NEA), the average annual teacher salary is $38,611. The 1997 American Federation of Teachers' (AFT) salary survey reports that the average beginning salary for a teacher with a bachelor's degree is $25,190. The average maximum salary for a teacher with a master's degree is $44,694.

Outlook

Teachers are generally in short supply across the nation due to rising school enrollments and the number of teachers who are retiring. The U.S. Department of Education predicts that one mil-

FOR MORE INFO

For more information on a teaching career, contact:
American Federation of Teachers
555 New Jersey Avenue, NW
Washington, DC 20001
Tel: 202-879-4400
Web: http://www.aft.org

National Education Association
1201 16th Street, NW
Washington, DC 20036
Tel: 202-833-4000
Web: http://www.nea.org

The following association offers a packet of information regarding careers in mathematics.
National Council of Teachers of Mathematics
Department M
1906 Association Drive
Reston, VA 20191
Tel: 703-620-9840
Web: http://www.nctm.org

lion new teachers will be needed by 2006. Math teachers are particularly needed. According to surveys conducted by AFT, school districts report a considerable shortage of math teachers, with greater shortages occurring in large cities.

Mathematicians

What Mathematicians Do

Mathematicians solve problems in higher mathematics, including algebra, geometry, number theory, and logic. *Theoretical mathematicians* develop new thoughts and ideas in mathematics. *Applied mathematicians* try to use these theories in practical ways.

Theoretical mathematicians usually teach in colleges and universities. They also work in the research departments of businesses or in government. Their theories are used in engineering, computer science, nuclear energy, space exploration, sociology, psychology, and education.

Applied mathematicians use mathematical theories to solve practical problems. They work in business, industry, or government. They solve problems ranging from the stability of rockets to the effects of new drugs. *Financial analysts* are applied mathematicians who make predictions about what sorts of investments will be profitable. *Computer-applications engineers* are applied mathematicians who solve scientific and engineering problems.

Though mathematicians work in all sorts of fields, they have certain things in common. First, they must enjoy mathematics and the challenge of solving problems. They must work logically, patiently, and imaginatively on these problems. Applied mathematicians must also understand the basic concepts of the business or profession they work in, whether it is engineering, economics, or sociology.

Education and Training

If you want to be a mathematician, you should concentrate on your math classes. In high school, you must take all the math that is offered. These courses will include algebra, geometry, trigonometry, and calculus. English composition and computer science classes are also important.

All mathematicians must have a least a bachelor's degree in mathematics from a four-year college. A master's degree is even more valuable, and you will need a doctorate for college-level teaching and more advanced research work.

EXPLORING

Ask your math teacher about competitions you can enter. For example, MATHCOUNTS is a national math coaching and competition program for seventh- and eighth-graders.

Students compete in one of more than 500 local meets in February. Winners then go to state contests in March. The national finals take place in May in Washington, DC. For more information, contact:

MATHCOUNTS
Foundation
1420 King Street
Alexandria, VA 22314
703-684-2828
http://mathcounts.org/

PROFILE:
GRACE HOPPER

When mathematician Grace Hopper (1906-1992) was young, her hobbies were needlepoint, reading, and playing the piano. Her father encouraged her to pursue things that interested her, even if they were considered more "masculine" pursuits. When she was 17, she entered Vassar College and she also studied at Yale.

Hopper wanted to join the military in World War II, but the government said she was too old at 34. She didn't stop trying, though, and in 1943, she was sworn into the U.S. Navy Reserve. She also managed to get special permission because she did not meet the weight requirement. She weighed only 105 pounds—16 pounds underweight for her height. She served in the navy for 43 years.

Hopper coined the term "bug," meaning a computer fault, while working on the Harvard Mark I computer. The real bug in the Mark I was a moth that caused a hardware problem.

In 1969 the Data Processing Management Association named her the first computer science "Man of the Year," and she was awarded the National Medal of Technology in 1991.

Earnings

Income varies with level of training and work setting. Mathematicians with bachelor's degrees in entry-level positions earn about $31,800 a year. Those with master's degrees earn about $38,300 a year. The average yearly salary for many mathematicians in the government is around $62,000 a year. Mathematical statisticians earn about $65,660. *Cryptanalysts* (mathematicians who decipher coding systems to transmit military, political, financial, or law enforcement information) earn $56,160.

Outlook

There will probably be more jobs in applied mathematics and related areas like computer programming, operations research, and engineering design than in theoretical research. Those who have a background in another field besides mathematics will have better chances of employment and advancement. The best opportunities for mathematicians with only a bachelor's degree will be in computer science. Those with bachelor's or master's degrees in mathematics who also meet state certification requirements can find jobs as high school math teachers.

FOR MORE INFO

For information on careers in mathematics, contact the following organizations.

Association for Women in Mathematics
4114 Computer and Space Sciences Building
University of Maryland
College Park, MD 20742-2461
Tel: 301-405-7892
Email: awm@math.umd.edu
Web: http://www.awm-math.org

Society for Industrial and Applied Mathematics
3600 University City Science Center
Philadelphia, PA 19104
Tel: 215-382-9800
Email: siam@siam.org
Web: http://www.siam.org

Operations
Research Analysts

Where Do They Work?

Major employers of operations research analysts are:

Manufacturers of machinery and transportation equipment

Telecommunications companies

Banks

Insurance companies

Private management consulting firms

The federal government, especially the armed forces

What Operations Research Analysts Do

Operations research analysts are problem solvers. They help companies work more smoothly and with less waste of time and money. They may, for example, help design the layout of a store or choose the best location for one. Or, they may figure out how an insurance company can introduce new customer services with the least cost and disruption.

The job duties of analysts vary depending on their employers, but all follow the same general steps in doing their work. First, company managers describe a business problem to the analyst. For example, a bank president might want to improve ways to process checks. He or she also might want to know which workers should be involved in each part of the system.

Analysts then make mathematical models of how checks are currently processed.

To do this, they divide the present system into steps. They give a number value to each step. Then analysts study the mathematical relationships between the steps. The model can be changed to figure out what will happen to the system under different conditions. Many models are computerized. Thus, analysts need to be able to use or write computer programs.

Analysts may take several weeks or months to solve a problem. They research the current system, evaluate it, and redesign it. Larger organizations may have systems that involve hundreds of employees in dozens of different departments.

Operations research analysts work for a variety of employers. These include manufacturers of machinery and transportation equipment, banks, telecommunications companies, insurance companies, and management consultants. The federal government, especially the armed forces, also hires analysts.

Operations research analysts often work as part of a research team consisting of other mathematicians and engineers, and they frequently use data-processing

EXPLORING

Visit the INFORMS Web site (see For More Information). It has career information, including profiles of operations research analysts and the work they do. Click on Education/Students and then Career Booklet. This site also lists magazines and educational opportunities.

LET'S GET TECHNICAL

Operations research analysts use **queuing theory** to study the flow of people or goods. Walt Disney World uses queuing theory to keep the lines moving at Space Mountain.

An operations research analyst uses **stochastic (random, chance) modeling** to predict the number and kind of personnel a company will need over a five-year period. Or it is used to schedule routes for airlines or police patrol cars.

Optimization is used to find the best way to meet certain requirements. For example, it helps determine how timber should be cut to minimize waste and maximize profits.

Source: Institute for Operations Research and the Management Sciences

equipment in their research. They prepare written and oral reports of their findings for upper-management officials.

Education and Training

School courses that can help you prepare for this career include mathematics, English composition, and computer science.

Some employers want analysts to have a bachelor's degree in mathematics, business administration (management), or operations research. Others expect employees to have master's degrees in one of these fields. More employers are looking for analysts with degrees in computer science, information science, or data processing. Analysts who work for the government usually have to pass a civil service examination.

New employees usually get several months of on-the-job training. Those with little or no experience work closely with experienced analysts during this period.

Earnings

Beginning analysts earn between $29,000 and $35,000 a year. Those with experience earn between $36,000 and $53,000 a year, depending on their job duties and the size of the company. Those with a lot of experience earn up to $90,000 per year or more. Those operations research analysts who work for the federal government usually receive lower salaries than those in private companies.

Outlook

The job outlook for operations research analysts is very good through the next 10 years. This is because companies that have used analysts to help make decisions have been very successful.

FOR MORE INFO

For more information about a career as an operations research analyst, contact:

American Mathematical Society
PO Box 6248
Providence, RI 02940
Tel: 401-455-4000
Web: http://www.ams.org

Institute for Operations Research and the Management Sciences (INFORMS)
901 Elkridge Landing Road, Suite 400
Linthicum, MD 21090-2909
Tel: 800-4INFORMS
Web: http://www.informs.org

Society for Industrial and Applied Mathematics
3600 University City Science Center
Philadelphia, PA 19104
Tel: 215-382-9800
Email: siam@siam.org
Web: http//www.siam.org

RELATED JOBS

Auditors
Business Managers
Cost Estimators
Management Analysts and Consultants
Risk Managers

Optical Engineers

What Optical Engineers Do

Optics is the study of light and how it interacts with matter. It is a branch of physics and engineering. *Optical engineers* use their knowledge of how light is produced, sent, detected, and measured to design such things as wireless communications, audio/CD players, high-definition television, laser printers, atomic research, robotics, and medical and scientific methods and tools.

Optical engineers may design optical systems for cameras, telescopes, or lens systems. They fine tune optical devices. They design and develop circuitry and parts for devices that use optical technology. These engineers may also design and test instruments that measure how well optical systems are working.

To create a new product using optical technology, optical engineers follow a process that has many steps. They study

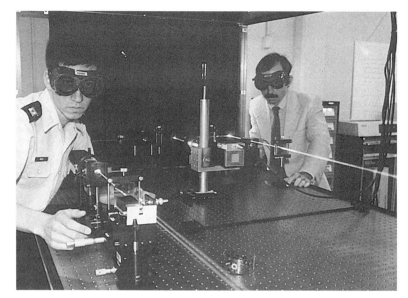

Optical engineers adjust a beam in a research laboratory. The beam will test optical and electro-optical devices that process and interpret communication signals.

the problem to understand it thoroughly. Then they use their imagination and training to come up with a solution for the problem. Once they have an idea, they turn it into a design or several designs. They use a computer to create a model, or they make a sample. They test the model or sample and change it as they find problems. They repeat this building and testing until they feel that their product is complete. The design is then sent to a company that manufactures it. Optical engineers often work on a team of engineers, industrial designers, technologists, and technicians.

Some optical engineers specialize in lasers and fiber optics. They are known as *fiber optics engineers* and *laser and*

EXPLORING

• Join science and engineering clubs that offer opportunities for experimentation, problem-solving, and teambuilding activities.
• Ask your teacher or a parent to help you perform simple experiments that examine the properties of light. Books on optics often provide instructions for experiments.
• Your teacher or librarian can help you find books and videos on optics.

fiber optics engineers. Fiber optics are thin, hair-like strands of plastic-coated glass fibers that transmit light and images. Lasers may be used to generate the light in these fibers. *Lasers are devices that produce thin,* powerful beams of light. They can be used in medical and surgical procedures, manufacturing, robotics, printing, and military systems, such as navigation systems and weapons systems. Fiber optics technology is used in sensors that detect temperature, pressure, and other physical features. This technology is also used in communications systems such as telephone systems, computer networks, and fiber optic imaging, which involves the use of fiber optics to transmit light or images.

Education and Training

You must have a bachelor of science degree in engineering to become an optical engineer. Many colleges offer classes in optics. Only a very small number of schools, though, offer degree programs in optical engineering. Most colleges offer degrees in a related field, such as electrical engineering or

SCIENTISTS SEE THE LIGHT

The study of the properties of light began during the 1600s when Galileo built telescopes to observe the planets and stars. Scientists, such as Sir Isaac Newton, conducted experiments and studies that contributed to the understanding of light and how it operates. Among Newton's many experiments was his work with prisms to break sunlight into a spectrum of colors. Important studies also were done by Christiaan Huygens, a Dutch physicist. He came up with a theory about the wave properties of light.

physics, with a specialization in optics. Most programs take four or five years to complete. Some colleges require internships or cooperative work programs during which you work at a related job for one to three semesters.

Many students receive master's degrees. Those who plan to work in research usually earn a doctoral degree.

Earnings

Entry-level optical engineers earn about $39,000 a year. Those engineers with 10 years of experience average about $55,000 a year and even more. The highest paid optical engineers earn as much as $89,000.

Outlook

Opportunities for optical engineers will be very good in the next decade. New uses for optics technology are discovered all the time. The use of fiber optics technology in telecommunications is increasing, which means more opportunities for engineers in com-

FOR MORE INFO

For information on careers and student membership, contact:
Lasers and Electro-Optics Society
c/o The Institute of Electrical and Electronics Engineers
PO Box 1331
445 Hoes Lane
Piscataway, NJ 08855-1331
Tel: 732-562-3892

To receive a directory of colleges or a career video, or for information on scholarships and student membership, contact:
SPIE—The International Society for Optical Engineering
PO Box 10
1000 20th Street
Bellingham, WA 98227-0010
Tel: 360-676-3290
Web: http://www.spie.org

For information on student membership, contact:
Optical Society of America
2010 Massachusetts Avenue, NW
Washington, DC 20036
Tel: 202-223-8130
Web: http://www.osa.org

puter, broadcasting, cable, and telephone industries. Optical engineers will also find jobs in the medical and defense fields.

Physicists

What Physicists Do

Physicists try to understand the laws of nature and learn how to use these laws in practical ways. Some teach in high schools and colleges, some work for the federal government, and some work for industrial laboratories. Wherever they work, physicists spend a great deal of time doing research, performing laboratory experiments, and studying the results.

Physicists are concerned with the special properties of matter (solids, liquids, and gases) and energy. *Theoretical physicists* try to understand how matter and energy work. For example, they may study electrical or nuclear energy, try to define the laws of each, and then write them up in mathematical formulas. *Experimental physicists* perform experiments that test exactly what various kinds of matter and energy do. Then they try to come up with practical ways to use them. For example, they may work in the communications industries, such as television, telephone,

Two physicists adjust a super-concentrating solar collector.

or radio to invent technologies for better pictures or better sound.

Physicists work in many areas. Some study atoms to learn the secrets of nuclear energy. Others work with engineers to find the best ways to build bridges and dams. Others conduct experiments for petroleum companies, to find better ways to obtain, refine, and use crude oil. Physicists are important to the space program. They try to figure out what outer space is actually like, and they design and test spaceships. Physicists often work with other scientists, such as chemists, biologists, and geologists. Biophysics and geophysics are two fields of science that were created when these scientists began to work together.

EXPLORING

• Ask your science teachers to assign some physics experiments.

• Join a science club or start one at your school.

• Enter a project in a science fair. If your school does not sponsor science fairs, you may find fairs sponsored by your school district, state, or a science society.

PHAMOUS PHYSICS LABS

These are some of the Department of Energy's research and development facilities.

Brookhaven National Laboratory in Upton, Long Island, New York, is mainly involved in studies of nuclear physics. It also does chemical, biological, electronic, and medical research.

Fermi National Accelerator Laboratory in Batavia, Illinois, conducts research in high-energy physics.

Lawrence Berkeley National Laboratory in Berkeley, California, conducts research in high-energy particle physics, nuclear fusion, computer-aided engineering, earth sciences, chemical sciences, and biological sciences.

Los Alamos National Laboratory in Los Alamos, New Mexico, conducts research in nuclear weapons and energy, cryogenic physics, space sciences, molecular biology, and metallurgy.

Physicists may specialize in mechanics, heat, optics (light), acoustics (sound), electricity and magnetism, electronics, particle physics (atoms and molecules), nuclear physics, or physics of fluids. All physicists must have keen powers of observation and a strong curiosity about the world around them.

Education and Training

There are some jobs available for physicists with only a bachelor's degree from a four-year college. If you have a bachelor's degree, you may be able to find a basic research job. If you have a teaching certificate, you can teach in secondary school.

Most physicists will need to go on for further education if they want to advance in the field. The more challenging and rewarding jobs go to physicists who have master's degrees and doctorates. Many of the most able physicists go on to complete postdoctoral education.

Earnings

Salaries for physicists range from about $35,000 a year to $76,000 a year or more. The most highly paid physicists have doctoral degrees and many years of experience.

Outlook

There will be fewer jobs for physicists through the year 2006. The best jobs will go to those with doctoral degrees. Physicists work in industry and research development laboratories. They also work as teachers and researchers at colleges and universities. Some physicists work for the federal government, mostly in the Departments of Commerce, Energy, and Defense.

FOR MORE INFO

For employment statistics and information on jobs and career planning, contact:
American Institute of Physics
Division of Careers Placement
One Physics Ellipse
College Park, MD 20740
Tel: 301-209-3100
Email: aipinfo@aip.org
Web: http://www.aip.org

For employment information, contact:
Canadian Association of Physics
Suite 112, MacDonald Building
150 Louis Pasteur Priv.
Ottawa, ON Canada KIN 6N5
Tel: 613-562-5614
Email: cap@physics.uottawa.ca
Web: http://www.cap.ca/

Fermilab offers internships, employment opportunities, and general information about their laboratory. Friends of Fermilab is a non-profit organization that supports precollege education programs.
Fermi National Accelerator Laboratory
PO Box 500
Batavia, IL 60510
Tel: 630-840-8258
Web: http://www.fnal.gov

Software Designers

What Software Designers Do

Without software, computers would not be able to work. Computers need to be told exactly what to do. Software is the set of codes that tells a computer what to do. It comes in the form of the familiar packaged software that you find in a computer store, such as games, word processing programs, spreadsheets, and desktop publishing programs. Software also comes in special forms designed for the specific needs of a particular business. *Software designers* create these software programs, also called applications. *Computer programmers* then create the software by writing the code that gives the computer instructions.

Software designers must imagine every detail of what a software application will do, how it will do it, and how it will look on the screen. An example is how a home accounting program is created. The software designer first decides what the pro-

A software designer gives instructions on how to use a new program.

gram should be able to do, such as balance a checkbook, keep track of incoming and outgoing bills, and keep records of expenses. For each of these tasks, the software designer decides what menus and icons to use, what each screen will look like, and whether there will be help or dialog boxes to assist the user. For example, the designer may want the expense record part of the program to produce a pie chart that shows the percentage of each household expense in the overall household budget. The designer can ask that the program automatically display the pie chart each time a budget is completed or only after the user clicks on a special icon on the toolbar.

Some software companies build custom-

EXPLORING

• **Learn as much as you can about computers. Keep up with new technology by reading computer magazines and by talking to other computer users.**
• **Join computer clubs.**
• **Use online services and the Internet for information about this field.**
• **Advanced students can put their design/ programming knowledge to work by designing and programming their own applications, such as simple games and utility programs.**

LIFE AS A SOFTWARE CONSULTANT

Cantrix Software Group Inc., in Chicago, Illinois, creates custom software applications using Microsoft tools. David Carpenter, president and founder, has been developing software since 1984. Before he started Cantrix in 1992, he held senior technical positions for companies such as AT&T and Motorola.

Carpenter has a bachelor's degree in computer science and engineering from the University of Illinois. He has taught Visual Basic and advanced C++ programming languages. He is also proficient in several other computer languages, including SQL, Ada, and C.

Carpenter says, "People who want to succeed in this field need to be focused, analytical, creative, and adaptable. If you are an independent learner, buy a PC and start teaching yourself a language like Microsoft Visual Basic. There are many resources on the World Wide Web to help you get started.

"Also, take the time in school to learn the craft of high-quality, well-designed software development, as opposed to the ad hoc, quick development that is so prevalent in the industry. It will pay high rewards."

designed software for the specific needs or problems of one business. Some businesses are large enough that they employ in-house software designers who create software applications for their computer systems.

Education and Training

Computer, science, and math classes will prepare you for a career as a software designer. In high school, you should take as many computer, science, and math courses as possible. English and speech classes help improve communication skills, which are important to software designers who make formal presentations to their managers and clients.

To be a software designer, you will need a bachelor's degree in computer science plus at least one year of experience with a programming language.

You also need knowledge of the field that you will be designing software for, such as education, business, or science. For example, someone with a bachelor s degree in computer science with a minor in business or accounting has an excellent chance for employment in creating business and accounting software.

Earnings

Salaries for software designers vary with the size of the company and with location. Software designers' salaries range from the $38,000 a year as a beginning designer to $51,000 a year as a senior designer or project team leader. Software design managers can earn $75,000 a year or more.

Outlook

Jobs in software design are expected to grow faster than the average through the year

FOR MORE INFO

Contact ACM for information on internships, student membership, and the ACM student magazine, Crossroads. ACM also has a student Web site at http://www.acm.org/membership/student/
Association for Computing Machinery (ACM)
1515 Broadway
New York, NY 10036-5701
Tel: 212-869-7440
Email: SIGS@acm.org
Web: http://www.acm.org

For information on scholarships, student membership, and the student newsletter, looking.forward, contact:
IEEE Computer Society
1730 Massachusetts Avenue, NW
Washington, DC 20036
Tel: 202-371-0101
Web: http://www.computer.org

2006, according to the U.S. Department of Labor. Employment of computing professionals is expected to increase as technology advances. The expanding use of the Internet by businesses has caused a growing need for skilled professionals.

Software Engineers

Where Do They Work?

Most software engineers are employed by computer and data processing companies and by consulting firms. Software engineers also work in:

Medicine

Industry

Military

Communications

Aerospace

Science

What Software Engineers Do

Businesses use computers to do complicated work for them. In many cases, their needs are so specialized that commercial software programs cannot perform the desired tasks. *Software engineers* change existing software or create new software to solve problems in many fields, including business, medicine, law, communications, aerospace, and science. For example, many software engineers are now working on projects to automate government and business forms. In the near future, it will be possible for almost everyone to fill out tax returns, insurance claims, and many other forms directly on the computer.

The projects software engineers work on are all different, but their methods for solving a problem are similar. First, engineers talk to clients to find out their needs and to define the problems they are having. Next, the engineers look at

the software already used by the client to see whether it could be changed or if an entirely new system is needed. When they have all the facts, software engineers use scientific methods and mathematical models to figure out possible solutions to the problems. Then they choose the best solution and prepare a written proposal for managers and other engineers.

Once a proposal is accepted, software engineers and technicians check with hardware engineers to make sure computers are powerful enough to run the new programs. The software engineers then outline program details. *Engineering technicians* write the initial version in computer languages.

EXPLORING

• Learn as much as you can about computers and computer software. Read computer magazines and talk to other computer users.

• Join computer clubs and surf the Internet for information about working in this field.

Throughout the programming process, engineers and technicians run diagnostic tests on the program to make sure it is working well at every stage. They also meet regularly with the client to make sure they are meeting their goals and to learn about any changes the client wants.

When a software project is complete, the engineer prepares a demonstration of it for the client. Software engineers might also install the program, train users, and make arrangements to help with any problems that arise in the future.

Education and Training

It is strongly recommended that you at least earn an associate's degree in computer technology. With an associate's degree, you can find a software engineering technician position. A bachelor's degree is required for most software engineers.

Another choice besides formal education at a technical/vocational school or university is commercial certification. Several large computer companies sponsor training and certification exams in many computing fields.

ADVICE FROM A PRO

On the Web site, JobProfiles.com, software engineer Bruce says education is key. "To program you must have an ability to group your thoughts into a logical pattern. But you have to learn the language you wish to code in and this takes time. Never give up. Start with the simple problems and move on up to the more complex ones. Find a good software company that is willing to take on individuals that are willing to be persistent in solving the problems. You won't always succeed but keep at it. In time it will start making sense and then the fun really begins. . . . There is a certain thrill in solving a problem with code and even more when one can go back later and see a faster way of doing it."

Source: http://www.jobprofiles.com

Earnings

Software engineering technicians usually earn beginning salaries of $24,000 a year. Computer engineers with a bachelor's degree in computer engineering earn starting salaries of $39,722 a year, according to the *Occupational Outlook Handbook.* New computer engineers with a master's degree earn $44,734, and those with a Ph.D. earn about $63,367. Experienced software engineers can earn more than $80,000 a year. Software engineers generally earn more in areas where there are lots of computer companies, such as the Silicon Valley in northern California.

Outlook

The need for software engineers will remain high, growing much faster than the average through 2006. Computer companies, consulting firms, major corporations, insurance agencies, banks, and other industries hire software engineers.

FOR MORE INFO

For more information, contact the following organizations:

Software & Information Industry Association
1730 M Street, NW, Suite 700
Washington, DC 20036-4510
Tel: 202-452-1600
Web: http://www.siia.net

Institute for Certification of Computing Professionals
2200 East Devon Avenue, Suite 247
Des Plaines, IL 60018
Tel: 847-299-4227
Web: http://www.iccp.org

Contact ACM for information on internships, student membership, and the ACM student magazine, Crossroads.
Association for Computing Machinery (ACM)
1515 Broadway
New York, NY 10036 5701
Tel: 212-869-7440
Email: SIGS@acm.org
Web: http://www.acm.org

RELATED JOBS

Computer Programmers
Computer Network Specialists
Database Specialists
Webmasters

Statisticians

You probably know Florence Nightingale (1820-1910) as a famous nurse and pioneer in British health care reform. Did you know that she was also a statistician? When she was serving as a nurse during the Crimean War, she collected data using statistical techniques to find out how many British soldiers died because of unsanitary hospital conditions. She used this information to show why hospital conditions needed to be changed. By doing this, Florence Nightingale showed how statistics can be used to improve medical and surgical practices.

What Statisticians Do

Statisticians use mathematics and statistical theory to collect and interpret information in a particular field. Statisticians work in almost every kind of occupational field, but most statisticians work in one of three kinds of jobs: they may teach and research at a university, they may work in a governmental agency (such as the Bureau of Census), or they may work in a business or industry. Some statisticians work for public opinion research companies. Their studies help us understand what different groups of people think about issues of the day.

Statisticians usually specialize in one of two areas. *Mathematical statisticians* think of new statistical methods and theories and create new ways to use these theories. *Applied statisticians* apply existing formulas to new questions. They may try to predict population growth or economic conditions, or estimate a crop yield.

Bob Rosenberg, official scorer for Major League Baseball's Chicago White Sox, readies his stat book for another game.

In some cases, statisticians actually go out and gather the statistics they need. However, usually such facts are gathered by people who are trained especially in fact-gathering techniques. In the Bureau of Census, for example, information is gathered by thousands of census takers. Once the census takers have gathered the information, it is given to statisticians. The statisticians then organize and analyze the information and make conclusions or recommendations about it.

Education and Training

Statisticians must have strong mathematics and computer backgrounds. In high school, you will need to take college preparatory classes in mathematics and computers.

EXPLORING

Ask your math teachers to show you a statistics textbook. They might be able to give you some simple statistical problems related to grades, for example. Or they might be able to arrange a visit to a local insurance agency, the local office of the Internal Revenue Service, or a nearby college to talk to people who use statistical methods.

WHAT DO SPORTS STATISTICIANS DO?

Sports statisticians compute and record the statistics on a particular sports event, game, or competition. They use basic math and algebra and calculators and computers.

Most high school, college, and professional sports teams have an official scorer/statistician who attends every home game and sits courtside, at what is called the scorer's table. The team scorer/statistician running stats at a basketball game, for example, keeps track of the score, the number of time-outs, and specific calls made by the referees, such as team and player fouls. The statistician is also called the *official scorer* because if any item on the scoreboard is questioned—by a referee, one of the coaches, or another game official—the statistician is the one who provides the answer.

Many statisticians still work by hand with a special notebook for recording the game statistics. As each play and call occurs in the game, the statistician writes down the play or call in a particular column or row of the stat book. Later, the statistician will add the total number of player errors, rebounds, assists, or goals. He or she can use these numbers to figure out such statistics as the average number of rebounds in a quarter or per game. Usually, the statistician keeps the stats for both the home team and the visiting team by individual. At the end of the game, the statistician can then provide both coaches and teams with specific information on their play during the game. Some statisticians use computers with specialized software programs that automatically compute the player and team statistics.

A bachelor's degree is the minimum education you need to work as a statistician. For many positions, though, you will need a master's or doctoral degree. In college, many students choose a major in mathematics, or in the field they hope to work in, such as chemistry or sociology.

Earnings

The average income for statisticians in the federal government in 1997 was $61,030 a year. Statisticians in private industry generally earn more than those who work for the federal government. Statisticians with higher educational degrees and more experience usually earn more than those with less education.

Statisticians who teach at colleges or universities earn salaries between $41,150 and $90,500 a year.

Outlook

Currently, there are about 14,000 statisticians in the United States. About one-fourth of them work for the federal government. The others work in industry or as teachers and researchers in colleges and universities. Jobs for statisticians can be found throughout the country, but most of them are in larger cities.

The number of jobs in this field is not expected to grow very much between now and the year 2006. However, statisticians with advanced degrees

FOR MORE INFO

For further information, contact:
American Statistical Association
1429 Duke Street
Alexandria, VA 22314-3402
Tel: 703-684-1221
Web: http://www.amstat.org

Society for Industrial and Applied Mathematics
3600 University City, Science Center
Philadelphia, PA 19104-2488
Tel: 215-382-9800
Web: http://www.siam.org

Association for Women in Mathematics
4114 Computer and Space Sciences Building
University of Maryland
College Park, MD 10742
Tel: 301-405-7892
Email: awm@math.umd.edu
Web: http://www.awm-math.org

and computer training should still be able to find jobs. Many of the current openings are in scientific and medical research.

Surveyors

Surveying Goes High-Tech

New technologies, such as the Global Positioning System, Geographic Information Systems (GIS), and remote sensing, allow surveyors to be more accurate and productive in their work. Surveyors can use remote sensors and satellite mapping to gather enormous amounts of information before they make the trip to an actual site.

What Surveyors Do

Surveyors use a variety of mechanical and electronic tools to measure exact distances and locate positions on the earth's surface. These geographic measurements are used in many ways. They determine property boundaries and provide information for mapmaking and construction and engineering projects. Wherever you need to find exact locations and measure points, surveyors make an accurate and detailed survey of the area.

Some surveyors work on proposed construction projects such as highways, airstrips, housing developments, and bridges to provide the necessary measurements before the engineers and construction crews begin work. Some help mapmakers chart unexplored areas. Others survey land claims, bodies of water, and underground mines. Some clear the right-of-way for water pipes, drainage ditches, or telephone lines. Some surveyors measure areas of land,

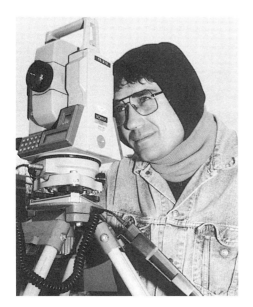

A surveyor checks the distance of an object.

sea, or space that are so large that their measurements must take into account the curvature of the earth. Some use special photographic equipment installed in airplanes or ground stations to chart areas that are hard to reach in person.

Whatever their area of specialization, surveyors must enjoy working outdoors in all kinds of weather. They must be comfortable with the mathematics necessary to make exact measurements. They must be able to work with a variety of mechanical and electronic measuring devices and have the leadership qualities to direct and supervise the work of people on their surveying team.

EXPLORING

Ask your school or community librarian to help you find books on the history and nature of surveying.

Learn all you can about these subjects:

• Information technology

• Mathematics

• Computers, computer graphics

• Satellite technology

• Working outdoors

• The environment

• Science

• Travel

WHAT DO SURVEYING AND MAPPING TECHNICIANS DO?

Surveying and mapping technicians help civil engineers, map-makers, and professional surveyors determine, describe, and record geographic areas and features.

Surveying and mapping technicians set up, adjust, and take readings from delicate surveying instruments. Some technicians adjust and operate instruments called *theodolites,* which measure vertical and horizontal angles of land or buildings. Technicians must hold certain rods in place so that the theodolite can be focused on the correct site, somewhat like an object that is viewed through a camera lens. Some technicians use equipment that electronically measures distances, or they may have to hand-hold measuring tape and chains. As readings are taken, the technicians must keep careful notes so that surveying reports will be accurate. They often enter the information from readings into computers.

Technicians may also do highway, pipeline, railway, or powerline surveying. Technicians who work for hydrographic surveying firms make surveys of harbors, rivers, and other bodies of water. These surveys help engineers to plan breakwaters, dams, locks, piers, and bridges.

Mining companies also use surveying and mapping technicians. These technicians use instruments that set the boundaries of mining claims and also show features of the earth that indicate the presence of valuable natural resources.

Topographical surveys show such features as mountains, lakes, forests, farms, and other landmarks. Technicians who do topographical surveying often take aerial and land photographs with special cameras that photograph large areas of land.

Education and Training: Surveying and mapping technicians must take a two-year program in surveying and mapping at a junior or technical school. Surveying firms often provide additional on-the-job training.

Earnings: The average yearly salary for full-time technicians is about $24,000 a year. Some earn as much as $48,000 a year.

Outlook: Job opportunities for surveying and mapping technicians should be good through the year 2006.

Education and Training

It is important to concentrate on math classes for a surveying career. In high school, you should take courses in algebra, geometry, physics, and mechanical drawing. After high school, you will have to complete a four-year college program in surveying or engineering. Civil engineering, with a surveying emphasis, is a common major. To advance in some of the more technical specialties, you may have to study beyond a bachelor's degree.

All 50 states require that land surveyors making property and boundary surveys be licensed or registered. If you work for the federal government, you must pass a civil service exam in addition.

Earnings

The median annual salary for surveyors is $36,000 a year. The average salary for registered land surveyors working for the federal government is

For more information about a career as a surveyor, contact

American Congress on Surveying and Mapping
5410 Grosvenor Lane, Suite 100
Bethesda, MD 20814
Tel: 301-493-0200

American Society for Photogrammetry and Remote Sensing
5410 Grosvenor Lane, Suite 210
Bethesda, MD 20814
Tel: 301-493-0290

about $47,000 a year. Surveyors with the most education and experience can earn up to $50,000.

Outlook

The employment outlook for surveyors is expected to be fairly good in the near future. Most will find jobs in private industry. About one-quarter will work for the federal government. Surveyors with the most education and training will be the most successful in finding good jobs.

Glossary

accredited: Approved as meeting established standards for providing good training and education. This approval is usually given by an independent organization of professionals to a school or a program in a school. Compare **certified** and **licensed**.

apprentice: A person who is learning a trade by working under the supervision of a skilled worker. Apprentices often receive classroom instruction in addition to their supervised practical experience.

apprenticeship: 1. A program for training apprentices (see apprentice). 2. The period of time when a person is an apprentice. In highly skilled trades, apprenticeships may last three or four years.

associate's degree: An academic rank or title granted by a community or junior college or similar institution to graduates of a two-year program of education beyond high school.

bachelor's degree: An academic rank or title given to a person who has completed a four-year program of study at a college or university. Also called an undergraduate degree or baccalaureate.

certified: Approved as meeting established requirements for skill, knowledge, and experience in a particular field. People are certified by the organization of professionals in their field. Compare **accredited** and **licensed**.

community college: A public two-year college, attended by students who do not live at the college. Graduates of a community college receive an associate degree and may transfer to a four-year college or university to complete a bachelor's degree. Compare **junior college** and **technical college**.

diploma: A certificate or document given by a school to show that a person has completed a course or has graduated from the school.

doctorate: An academic rank or title (the highest) granted by a graduate school to a person who has completed a two- to three-year program after having received a master's degree.

fringe benefit: A payment or benefit to an employee in addition to regular wages or salary. Examples of fringe benefits include a pension, a paid vacation, and health or life insurance.

graduate school: A school that people may attend after they have received their bachelor's degree. People who complete an educational program at a graduate school earn a master's degree or a doctorate.

intern: An advanced student (usually one with at least some college training) in a professional field who is employed in a job that is intended to provide supervised practical experience for the student.

internship: 1. The position or job of an intern (see intern). 2. The period of time when a person is an intern.

junior college: A two-year college that offers courses like those in the first half of a four-year college program. Graduates of a junior college usually receive an associate degree and may transfer to a four-year college or university to complete a bachelor's degree. Compare **community college.**

liberal arts: The subjects covered by college courses that develop broad general knowledge rather than specific occupational skills. The liberal arts are often considered to include philosophy, literature and the arts, history, language, and some courses in the social sciences and natural ciences.

licensed: Having formal permission from the proper authority to carry out an activity that would be illegal without that permission. For example, a person may be licensed to practice medicine or to drive a car. Compare **certified**.

major: (in college) The academic field in which a student specializes and receives a degree.

master's degree: An academic rank or title granted by a graduate school to a person who has completed a one- or two-year program after having received a bachelor's degree.

pension: An amount of money

paid regularly by an employer to a former employee after he or she retires from working.

private: 1. Not owned or controlled by the government (such as private industry or a private employment agency). 2. Intended only for a particular person or group; not open to all (such as a private road or a private club).

public: 1. Provided or operated by the government (such as a public library). 2. Open and available to everyone (such as a public meeting).

regulatory: Having to do with the rules and laws for carrying out an activity. A regulatory agency, for example, is a government organization that sets up required procedures for how certain things should be done.

scholarship: A gift of money to a student to help the student pay for further education.

social studies: Courses of study (such as civics, geography, and history) that deal with how human societies work.

starting salary: Salary paid to a newly hired employee. The starting salary is usually a smaller amount than is paid to a more experienced worker.

technical college: A private or public college offering two- or four-year programs in technical subjects. Technical colleges offer courses in both general and technical subjects and award associate degrees and bachelor's degrees.

technician: A worker with specialized practical training in a mechanical or scientific subject who works under the supervision of scientists, engineers, or other professionals. Technicians typically receive two years of college-level education after high school.

technologist: A worker in a mechanical or scientific field with more training than a technician. Technologists typically must have between two and four years of college-level education after high school.

undergraduate: A student at a college or university who has not yet received a degree.

undergraduate degree: See **bachelor's degree**.

union: An organization whose members are workers in a particular industry or company. The union works to gain better wages, benefits, and working conditions for its members. Also called a labor union or trade union.

vocational school: A public or private school that offers training in one or more skills or trades. Compare **technical school**.

wage: Money that is paid in return for work done, especially money paid on the basis of the number of hours or days worked.

Index of Job Titles

Math on the Web

A+ Math
http://www.aplusmath.com/

AllMath
http://www.allmath.com/

Aunty Math
http://www.dcmrats.org/AuntyMath.html

Cool Tools: Kids 'n Money
http://www.cyberinvest.com/cooltools/cooltools.kidsandmoney.html

Investing for Kids
http://library.thinkquest.org/3096/

Just for Middle School Kids: Math
http://www.westnet.com/~rickd/Kids/Math.html

Kids & Money
http://www.ext.nodak.edu/extnews/pipeline/d-parent.htm

KidsMath.com
http://www.kidsmath.com/

Kids Web: Math
http://www.kidsvista.com/Sciences/math.html

Money Cents
http://www.kidsmoneycents.com/

Money Matters for Kids
http://www.mmforkids.org/

U.S. Treasury's Page for Kids
http://www.ustreas.gov/kids/